Math
Puzzles Galore

Written by Rik Carter

Published by World Teachers Press®

Order Number 2-5156
ISBN 978-1-58324-083-0

F G H I J 11 10 09 08 07

395 Main Street
Rowley, MA 01969
www.didax.com

Foreword

Math Puzzles Galore is a blackline master book with 50 pages of problem-solving activities for students. They will help students organize their thoughts and working habits. The activities cover the important curriculum areas of:

- number
- measurement
- space

The activities can be done in any order and can be used in learning centers, as part of a whole-class activity, in small groups and for homework.

Many of the activities require few or no concrete materials apart from scissors or colored pencils.

Contents

Teachers Notes	4	Dividing Circles	30
Square Number Puzzle	5	Os and Xs	31
Paper Squares	6	Eight Circles	32
Addition Cross	7	Numbers and Squares	33
Squares and Squares	8	Lines and Xs	34
Square Jigsaw	9	Five-by-Five Magic	35
Every Room	10	Cube Models	36
Houses and Paths	11	Joining Numbers	37
Tracing Squares	12	Adding in Squares	38
Dividing Shapes	13	Adding Primes	39
Amazing Addition	14	Consecutive Letters	40
Shape Puzzle	15	Patterns and Shapes	41
Five and Four Squares	16	Numbers and Paths	42
Seven and Five Squares	17	Paint Problem	43
Large Magic Squares	18	Cut and Make	44
Four Cubes	19	Paper Run	45
A Magic Hexagon	20	Going in Circles	46
What a Diamond!	21	Number Placement	47
Number Paths	22	Major Magic	48
Grid Coloring	23	Easy Addition	49
Consecutive Numbers	24	Adding Digits	50
Nine Squares	25	Triangle Addition	51
Time Addition	26	Make a Square	52
Octagon and Rectangle	27	Hexagon Magic	53
Squares and Paths	28	Minimum Colors	54
Dividing Shapes	29	Answers	55-56

Teachers Notes _____

Mathematics involves observing, representing and investigating patterns and relationships. This book provides students with opportunities to learn about mathematics, what it is and how it can be used in making decisions and solving problems. *Math Puzzles Galore* provides you with the resource to develop and enhance problem-solving skills in your students.

Some benefits of developing problem-solving strategies

1. None of us know what the future holds for our students; therefore, we need to prepare them for any situation they may encounter. It is no longer enough to provide students with a basic knowledge of number, space and measurement. They need to have the skills to use all areas of mathematics to develop a satisfactory solution to any problem they may encounter.

2. Students also need to be able to draw on the knowledge they already have and transfer it to an unfamiliar situation to help them solve a problem. They may need to access information not previously dealt with, and by having problem-solving skills as a base, students will be able to make the transition from a familiar problem to an unfamiliar one with relative ease.

3. Students may be required in the future to convey mathematical ideas to others. This will require a greater understanding of mathematics and an ability to solve problems. Students will need to work out the most efficient way to convey the ideas to ensure a full understanding is obtained.

4. We all encounter problems in our everyday life, such as calculating, when we are shopping, whether it is better value for money to purchase the large or the medium box of breakfast cereal. Developing problem-solving skills in our students will make their day-to-day mathematical problems far easier to solve.

Suggested lesson development

1. Select a page from the workbook and photocopy enough for each student in your class.

2. Provide an example on the board to work through with the class as a demonstration of the strategies that may be used when solving the problem for themselves. Encouraging students to work collaboratively in this way provides the less able with an idea of where to begin and how possibly to solve the problem. It also provides the other students with approaches they may never have thought of.

3. Once the example on the board is solved, hand out the worksheet to each student. Explain that the strategies previously discussed—or any other strategies they can develop—can be applied to this problem. Allow students adequate time to solve the problem.

4. Follow-up the activity with a sharing session in small groups. Each student can share his/her strategies with the group. Each group can then report back to the whole class on how they solved the problem.

5. Answers have been provided to ensure students are solving the problems correctly. Even though it is important to focus on the strategy or strategies used to solve the problems, it is equally important that students arrive at the correct solution.

Further development

1. Completion of all activities in *Math Puzzles Galore* will aid in the development of a broad range of strategies in problem solving.

2. Creating an awareness of problems in day-to-day experiences and providing opportunities for discussion of strategies and possible solutions will make students aware of the transfer of their knowledge into their everyday world.

Square Number Puzzle

Write the digits 1 to 9 in the squares below. You may use each digit only once. All the equations going across and the equation going down must be correct.

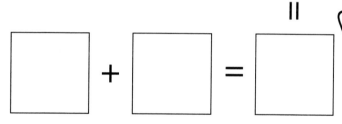

Can you rearrange the digits and equations to form another puzzle like the one above?

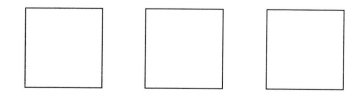

A square which has been divided into sixteen smaller squares can be cut exactly in half in six different ways.
Two of the ways have been done for you below.
Can you divide the four squares below into halves to show the other four methods?

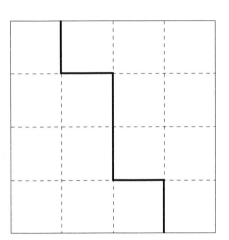

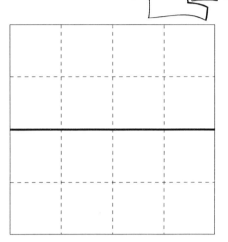

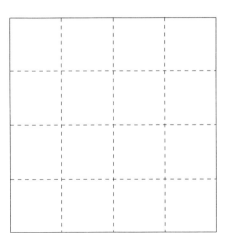

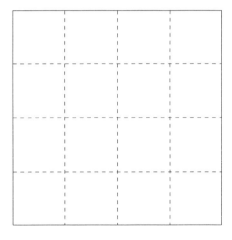

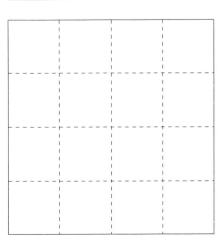

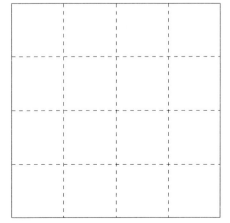

Arrange the numbers 2 to 10 in the cross below so that the horizontal and vertical totals are equal to 32.

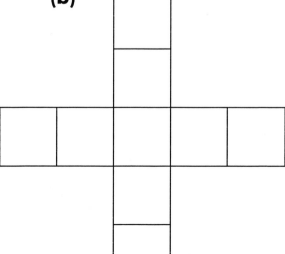

(a)

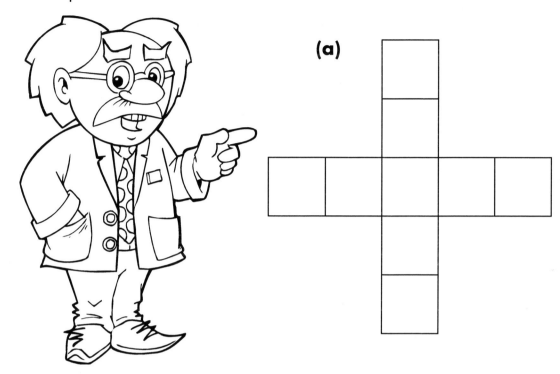

Using the same numbers as above with the crosses below, make one cross add up to 30 and the other to 28.

(b)

(c)

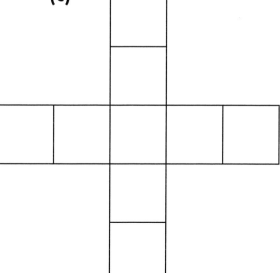

A square can easily be cut into four smaller squares.

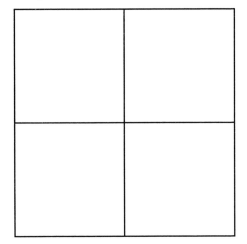

It is a little more difficult to cut a square into six smaller squares.

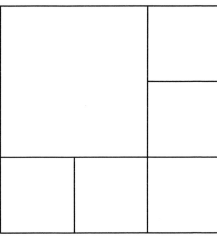

Can you cut the squares below into seven and then eight smaller squares?

www.worldteacherspress.com   © World Teachers Press®

Cut out the shapes below.
Put them together to make a square.

Every Room

Below is a plan of a house that has nine rooms.
Can you walk through each of the nine rooms by
crossing every wall just once?

5

3

2

4

1

6

7

8

9

www.worldteacherspress.com   © World Teachers Press®

Houses and Paths

Below is a map of five houses joined by nine paths. Start at the first house and try to walk to all the other houses using each path only once. Can you do this?

You must remember to use *all* the paths, but only *once*.

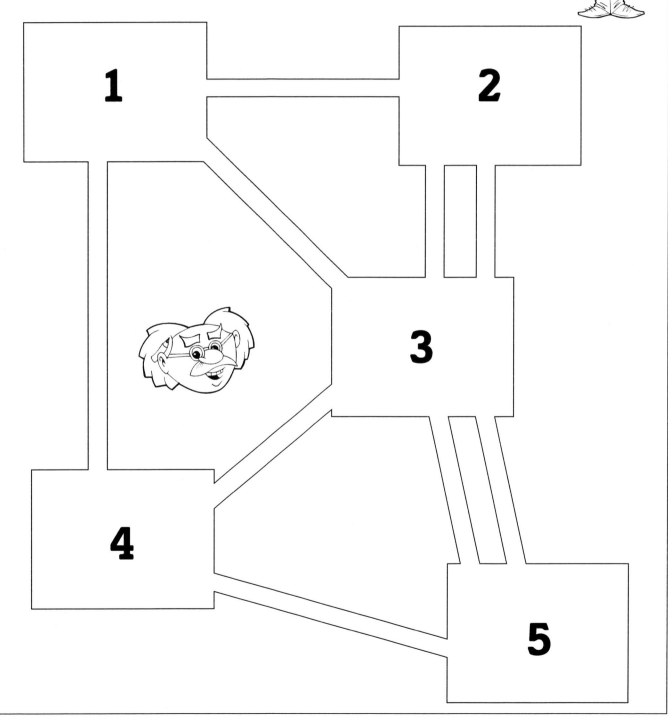

Tracing Squares

Trace over the diagram below, starting from the dot, without lifting your pencil from the paper and without tracing over the same line twice.

www.worldteacherspress.com   © World Teachers Press®

Dividing Shapes

Divide the shape below into two, three and four identical pieces.

Two identical pieces

Three identical pieces

Four identical pieces

Amazing Addition

Using colored pencils, try to find ways into the center of the maze that add up to:

16;
25; and
31.

What other totals can you come up with?

_____   _____   _____

_____   _____   _____

Shape Puzzle

Cut out the shapes below.
Rearrange them to make:

a square; and
a triangle.

Make five squares using toothpicks as shown below.
Move only two toothpicks to reduce the number of squares from five to four.
Toothpicks cannot overlap or be removed.

Seven and Five Squares

Make seven squares using toothpicks as shown below.
Move only three toothpicks to reduce the number of squares from seven to five.
Toothpicks cannot overlap or be removed.

Large Magic Squares

Put the numbers 2, 3, 5, 8, 9, 12, 14 and 15 into the empty squares so that all the rows, columns and large diagonals add up to 34.

	11	6	
4			13
	7	10	
16			1

Put the numbers 2, 5, 7, 8, 11, 12, 14 and 17 into the empty squares so that all the rows, columns and large diagonals add up to 38.

10			9
	15	4	
6			13
	3	16	

Put the numbers 9, 12, 18, 27, 30, 39, 45 and 48 into the empty squares so that all the rows, columns and large diagonals add up to 114.

	36	21	
15			42
	24	33	
51			6

Four Cubes

Eight completely different objects can be made using four cubes. Each cube must be joined to another cube along at least one face. Turning, flipping, or sliding a model does not make a new model. The four objects below are, in fact, only one answer.

Draw all eight answers in the boxes below.

A Magic Hexagon

Place the numbers 14 to 26 in the circles so that all the lines leading into the center add up to 60.

What a Diamond!

Place eight of the numbers from 1 to 9 into the small diamonds below so that if you add the numbers:

- around the big diamond;
- around the small diamond;
- along the straight line across the diamonds; and
- along the straight line down the diamond;

your total will be 20 each time. (You may use each number only once.)

Number Paths

Join the numbers horizontally or vertically so that you make a continuous path connecting twelve numbers that add up to 174.

Make up your own paths and share them with other people.

16	12	17	11	15
13	18	10	14	12
17	11	18	11	16
10	17	12	16	10
16	12	15	13	17

 www.worldteacherspress.com © World Teachers Press®

Grid Coloring

Color twelve of the squares in the grid below so that:

- there are no more than two per column;
- there are no more than two per row; and
- there are no more than two per diagonal.

<table>
<tr><td></td><td></td><td></td><td></td><td></td><td></td></tr>
<tr><td></td><td></td><td></td><td></td><td></td><td></td></tr>
<tr><td></td><td></td><td></td><td></td><td></td><td></td></tr>
<tr><td></td><td></td><td></td><td></td><td></td><td></td></tr>
<tr><td></td><td></td><td></td><td></td><td></td><td></td></tr>
<tr><td></td><td></td><td></td><td></td><td></td><td></td></tr>
</table>

Consecutive Numbers

Place the numbers 11 to 18 into the circles below so that no two consecutive numbers are in circles joined by a line.

Nine Squares

In the grid below, draw five shapes each with an area of nine squares. The shapes must have the following perimeters:

- Shape 1   Perimeter = 12;   • Shape 4   Perimeter = 18;
- Shape 2   Perimeter = 14;   and
- Shape 3   Perimeter = 16;   • Shape 5   Perimeter = 20.

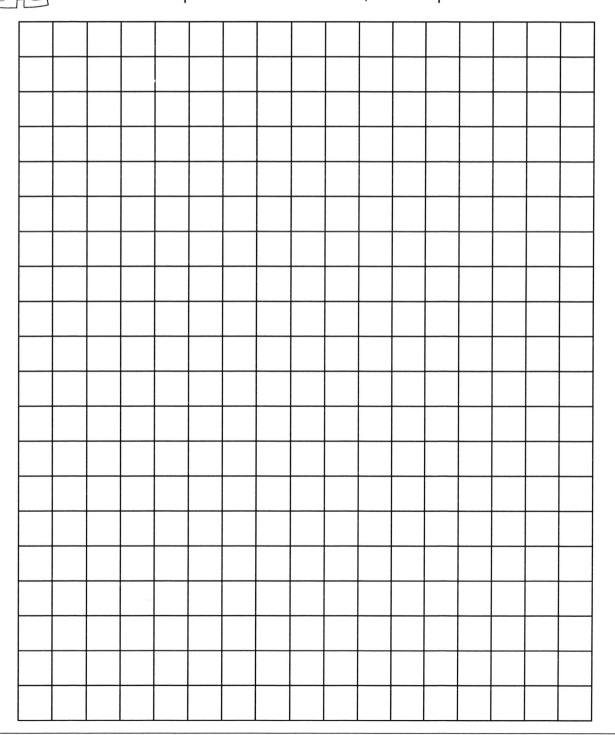

Use one straight line to divide the clock face below into two regions so that the sum of the numbers in each region is the same.

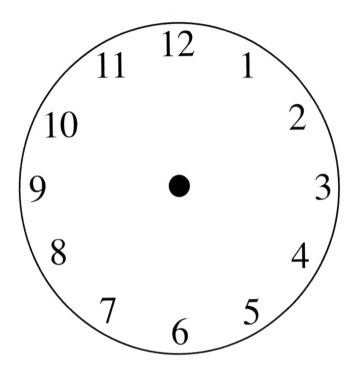

Use two straight lines to divide the clock face below into three regions so that the sum of the numbers in each region is the same.

Octagon and Rectangle

Cut out the shapes below
and rearrange them to make
a rectangle and an octagon.

Squares and Paths

Join the squares along the top to their matching squares with lines.

However, no lines may cross over another and you may not go outside the large square.

A   B   C   D

D   A

C

B

www.worldteacherspress.com   © World Teachers Press®

Divide the shape below into four.
Each quarter should be the same
size and shape.

Divide the shape below into four. Each quarter should be the same size and
shape.

Dividing Circles

Split the circle into two regions so that the sum of the numbers in each region is the same.

Split the circle into four regions so that the sum of the numbers in each region is the same.

www.worldteacherspress.com © World Teachers Press®

Os and Xs

Place ten Os and six Xs on the grid below so that the rows and columns that are eight squares long each have two Os and one X in them.

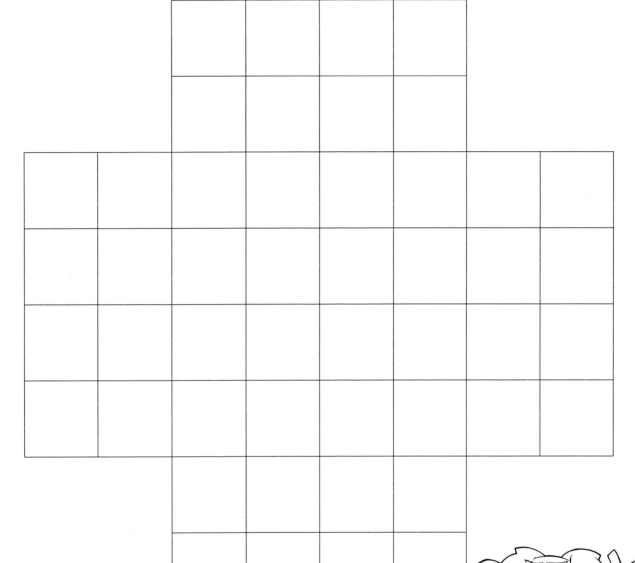

Eight Circles

Draw eight circles on the grid to the right so that:

- every circle is in a different square;
- there are no circles on the large diagonals of the grid; and
- there is only one circle in a row and column.

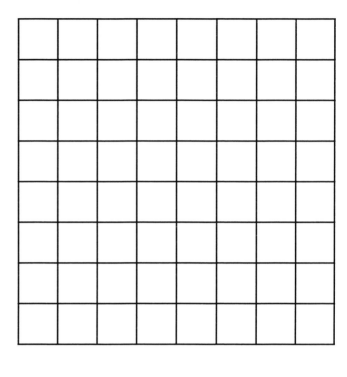

Draw eight circles on the grid below so that:

- every circle is in a different square;
- there are no circles on the large diagonals of the grid;
- no circle shares any diagonal; and
- there is only one circle in a row and column.

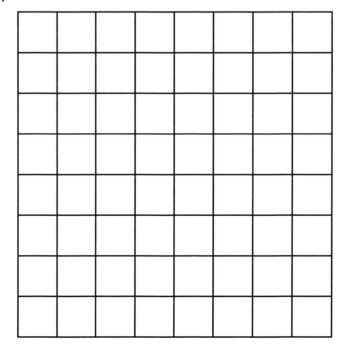

www.worldteacherspress.com   © World Teachers Press®

Numbers and Squares

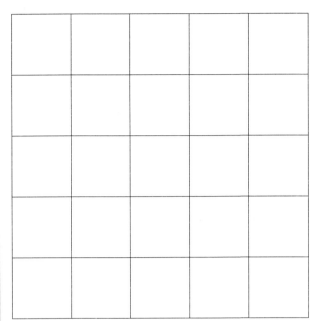

Place the numbers 1, 2, 3, 4 and 5 into the grid so that each number appears in all rows, columns and large diagonals. You will need to use each number five times.

Place the numbers 1, 2, 3, 4, 5, 6 and 7 into the grid so that each number appears in all rows, columns and large diagonals. You will need to use each number seven times.

Lines and Xs

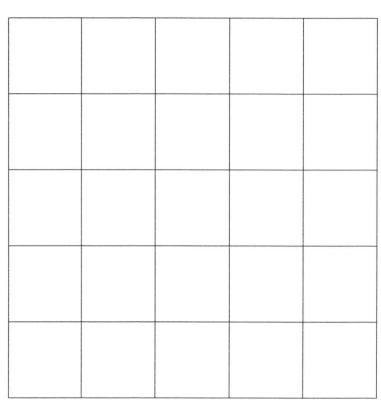

Place nine Xs on the grid so that you can draw eight straight lines that each join three Xs.

Rearrange the nine Xs on the grid so that you can draw nine straight lines that each join three Xs.

Five-by-Five Magic

Complete the magic square by placing the remainder of the numbers from 1 to 25 in the squares so that each column, row and large diagonal adds up to 65.

	24		8	15
	5			
		13		22
10	12	19		
		25	2	9

Complete the magic square by placing the remainder of the numbers from 13 to 37 in the squares so that each column, row and large diagonal adds up to 125.

29	36		20	
			26	
16		25		
		31	33	15
23	30	37		

www.worldteacherspress.com

Cube Models

How many cubes did it take to make the models below?

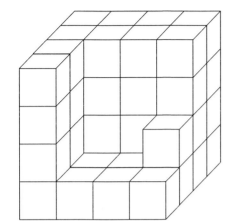

Model 1 took _____ cubes.

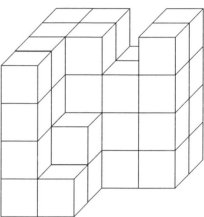

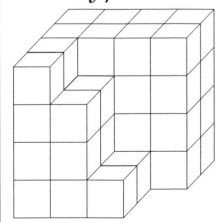

Model 2 took _____ cubes.

Model 3 took _____ cubes.

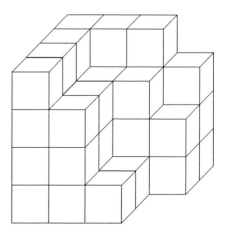

Model 4 took _____ cubes.

www.worldteacherspress.com

Joining Numbers

Join the number 1 to 1, 2 to 2, 3 to 3 and so on with straight lines along the grid. You must join all the numbers to their matching number but none of the paths may cross over.

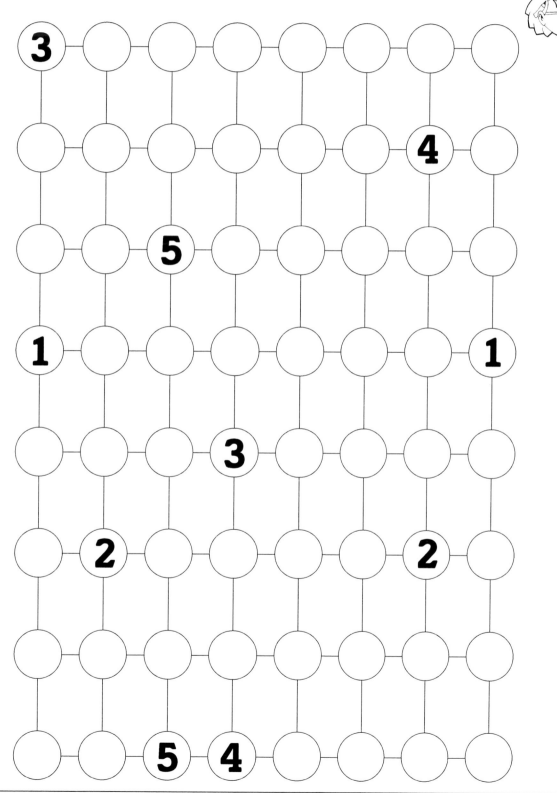

Adding in Squares

The four numbers in the grid have been added horizontally, vertically and diagonally. The answer to each addition sum has been written outside the grid.

The same has been done for the grids below. Can you find the numbers that need to be placed inside the grids?

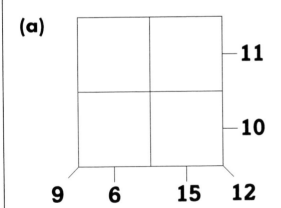

(a)

— 11
— 10

9   6   15   12

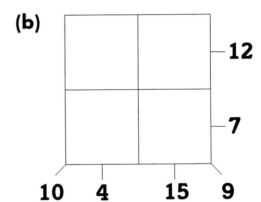

(b)

— 12
— 7

10   4   15   9

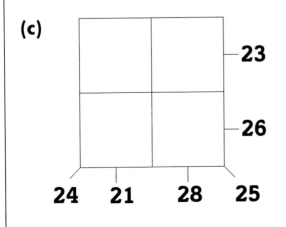

(c)

— 23
— 26

24   21   28   25

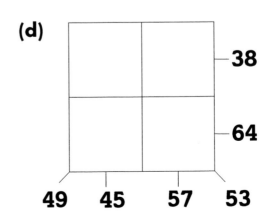

(d)

— 38
— 64

49   45   57   53

Adding Primes

Place all the prime numbers between 4 and 25 into the diagram below once, so that each of the columns and diagonals adds up to the same prime number.

What is the prime number? _____

Consecutive Letters

Place the letters A, B, C, D and E into the squares so that no two connected squares contain consecutive letters. For example, A cannot be connected to B.

Try to find four different solutions.

Patterns and Shapes

Cut out the nine shapes below and rearrange them in the grid so that:
- no row or column has more than one similar shape; and
- no row or column has more than one type of shading.

Numbers and Paths

Join the number 1 to 2 with a line.
Then do the same for 3 and 4, 5 and 6 and 7 and 8.

None of the lines may cross over each other.

1	4	2
	5	
	3	
7	6	8

Paint Problem

All the regions in the diagram below have an area of 8 cm², apart from the larger region at the bottom which has an area of 16 cm².

You have only enough paint to paint the following areas:
- 16 cm² of blue;
- 24 cm² of yellow;
- 16 cm² of red; and
- 16 cm² of green.

Paint the diagram so that no two touching areas are the same color. Two diagrams are provided as you will probably need them!

Cut and Make

Cut out the shapes below and rearrange them to make:
- a rectangle;
- a square;
- a triangle; and
- a parallelogram.

www.worldteacherspress.com © World Teachers Press®

Paper Run

The map below is not to scale. It represents a newspaper printing press, marked by the * and seven stores that sell newspapers, marked by the letters A to F. Find the shortest route that could be taken to deliver newspapers to all the stores by starting and finishing at the printing press.

How many kilometers is this route? _____

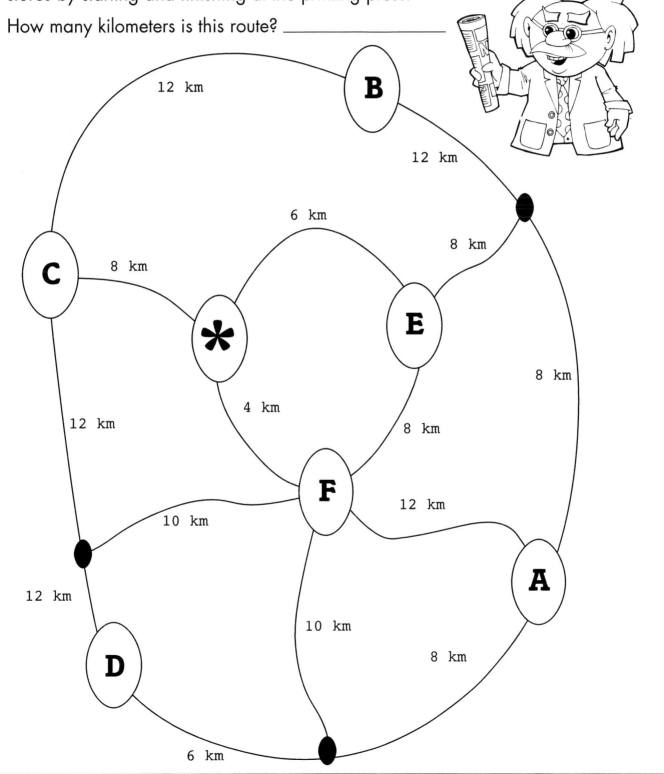

Going in Circles

Write the numbers 1 to 19 in the circles so that any three numbers joined by a straight line add up to the same number.

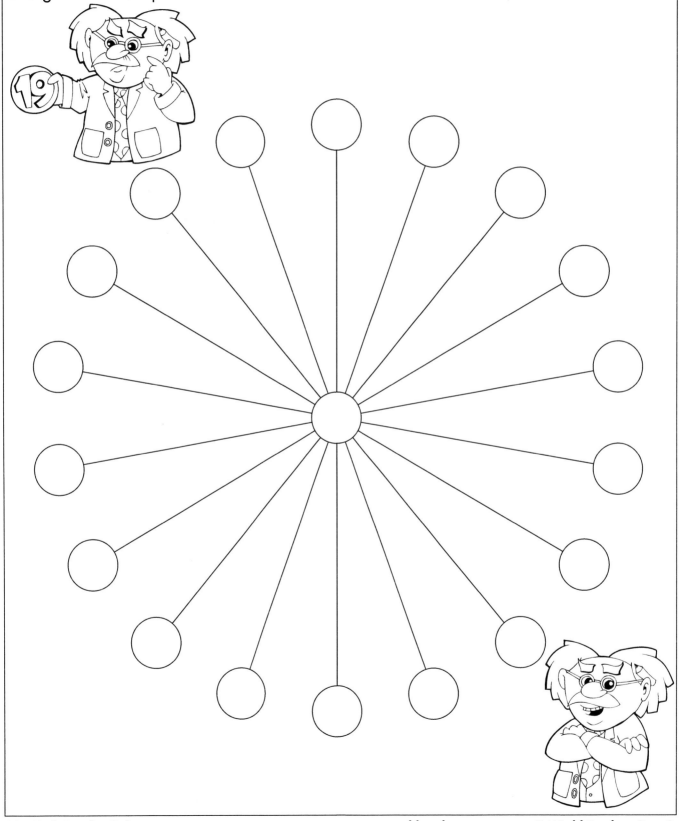

  www.worldteacherspress.com   © World Teachers Press®

Place the numbers 11 to 19 in the grid below. Use each number only once. You must also use the following rules:

- Row A has all even numbers;
- Row B has all odd numbers;
- 12 and 16 are in the same column;
- 16 is not in the same row as 14; and
- 11 and 19 are in the same row.

Columns

	A	B	C	Totals
A				44
B				45
C				46
Totals	44	45	46	54

Rows

Totals

Major Magic

Put the four squares together to make a 6 x 6 large magic square. Remember a magic square is one where the totals of each column, row and large diagonal add up to the same total or magic number.
You may need to try many combinations.

What is the magic number? _____

49	8	21
2	41	30
45	12	17

43	14	15
6	37	34
47	10	19

1	42	29
48	9	20
5	38	33

7	36	35
44	13	16
3	40	31

www.worldteacherspress.com   © World Teachers Press®

Easy Addition

In the grid below, the numbers go from 2 to 144 in multiples of 2.

How many numbers appear on the grid? _____

What is the sum of all the numbers? _____

Hint: There is an easy way of doing this.

2	4	6	8	10	12	14	16
18	20	22	24	26	28	30	32
34	36	38	40	42	44	46	48
50	52	54	56	58	60	62	64
66	68	70	72	74	76	78	80
82	84	86	88	90	92	94	96
98	100	102	104	106	108	110	112
114	116	118	120	122	124	126	128
130	132	134	136	138	140	142	144

Adding Digits

Arrange the digits 1 to 9 into the squares to form a correct addition problem.

One answer is provided. Can you make up another four?

Triangle Addition

Place the numbers 5, 10, 15, 20, 25, 30, 35, 40, 45, 50, 55 and 60 into the circles to make each line in the two triangles add up to 130.

Make a Square

Cut out the shapes below and put them together to make one large square.

www.worldteacherspress.com © World Teachers Press®

Place the numbers 1 to 19 into the hexagons so that each of the 15 rows adds up to 38.

What is the minimum number of colors required to color each of the diagrams below, so that no two touching areas have the same color?

www.worldteacherspress.com © World Teachers Press®

Answers

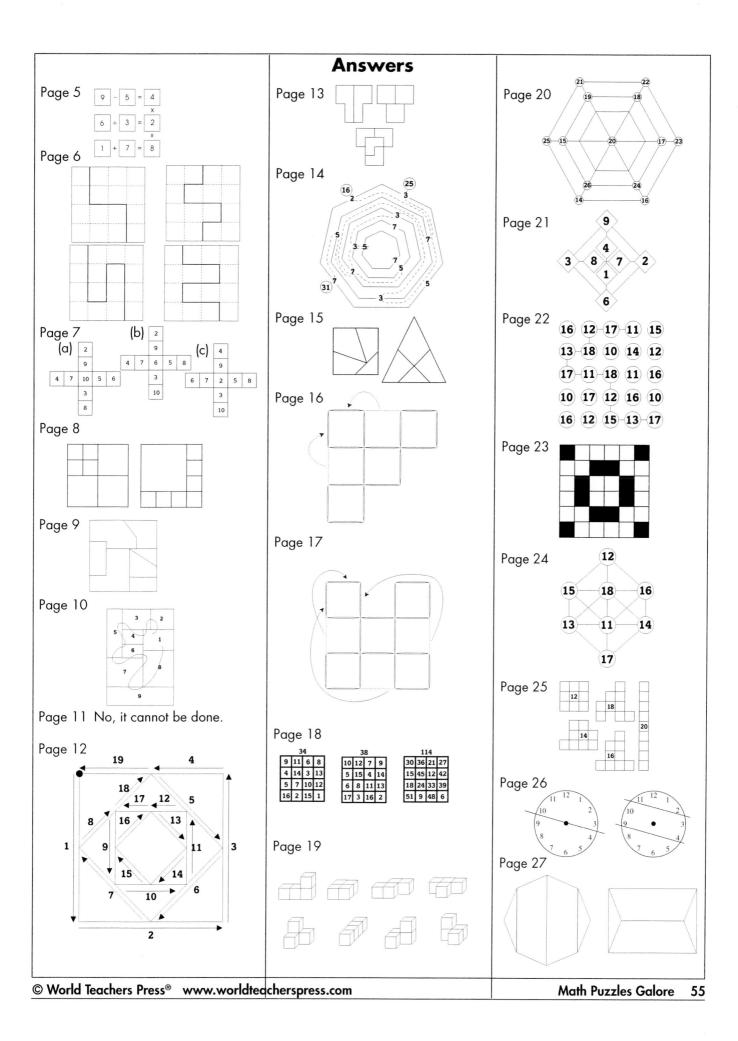

Page 5

Page 6

Page 7 (a) (b) (c)

Page 8

Page 9

Page 10

Page 11 No, it cannot be done.

Page 12

Page 13

Page 14

Page 15

Page 16

Page 17

Page 18

34			
9	11	6	8
4	14	3	13
5	7	10	12
16	2	15	1

38			
10	12	7	9
5	15	4	14
6	8	11	13
17	3	16	2

114			
30	36	21	27
15	45	12	42
18	24	33	39
51	9	48	6

Page 19

Page 20

Page 21

Page 22

Page 23

Page 24

Page 25

Page 26

Page 27

Answers

Page 28

Page 29

Page 30

Page 31

Page 32 - There are other answers

Page 33

1	2	3	4	5
4	5	1	2	3
2	3	4	5	1
5	1	2	3	4
3	4	5	1	2

1	2	3	4	5	6	7
6	7	1	2	3	4	5
4	5	6	7	1	2	3
2	3	4	5	6	7	1
7	1	2	3	4	5	6
5	6	7	1	2	3	4
3	4	5	6	7	1	2

Page 34

Page 35

17	24	1	8	15
23	5	7	14	16
4	6	13	20	22
10	12	19	21	3
11	18	25	2	9

29	36	13	20	27
35	17	19	26	28
16	18	25	32	34
22	24	31	33	15
23	30	37	14	21

Page 36
Model 1 = 47; Model 2 = 41;
Model 3 = 48; Model 4 = 43;

Page 37

Page 38

(a)
4	7	11
2	8	10
9	6	15	12

(b)
3	9	12
1	6	7
10	4	15	9

(c)
10	13	23
11	15	26
24	21	28	25

(d)
17	21	38
28	36	64
49	45	57	53

Page 39
The prime number is 41.

Page 40

Page 41

Page 42

Page 43

Page 44

Page 45

84 km

Page 46

Page 47

	A	B	C	Totals
A	18	12	14	44
B	15	17	13	45
C	11	16	19	46
Totals	44	45	46	54

Page 48

1	42	29	7	36	35
48	9	20	44	13	16
5	38	33	3	40	31
43	14	15	49	8	21
6	37	34	2	41	30
47	10	19	45	12	17

Magic Number – 150

Page 49
72 numbers appear on the grid.
36 number pairs, 2 + 144 = 146,
4 + 142 = 146 etc.
Total is 146 x 36 = 5,256.

Page 50 - Answers will vary.

Page 51

Page 52

Page 53

Page 54
For the square you need three colors.
For the circle you need four colors.

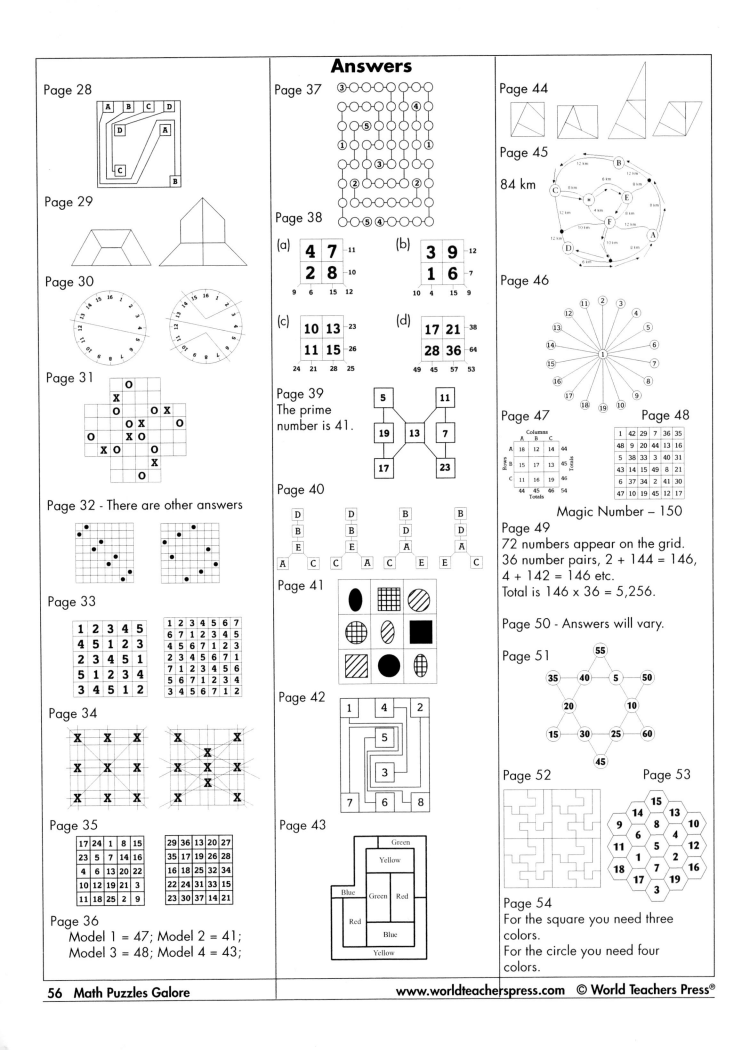